17 Prehistoric Monsters

Everyone Should Know About

Stanton F. Fink

Volume XI of Stanton's Coloring books

Acknowledgments

and Dedication

To my father, in whose books I discovered my first monsters.

To Will Caligan, whose help and encouragement is one of the primary reasons for this coloring book's existence.

To Mariano Silvera, who should have had his own artbooks

To Doctor David Morafka, who helped teach me to be more picky with my information.

To my friends, who helped push me to make this.

Table of Contents

Introduction

The purpose of this coloring book series is to provide information on various prehistoric animals both profoundly famous and incredibly obscure to artists of all ages. Of course, there is a lot of material to work with, as animals have been a major component of Earth's ecosystems for at least 670 million years.

For the sake of space and workability, each volume will contain 17 entries: ideally, one species for each geological time period, if possible. If you, or your inner and or outer child do not see your favorite prehistoric animal here, it may be eventually featured in another volume. Or, contact me to have it put into a later volume.

Glossary

- **Aquatic**- Living in water.
- **Arthropod**- Any member of the animal phylum Arthropoda, including trilobites, arachnids, crustaceans, insects, myriapods and their relatives. All arthropods have armor-like, jointed exoskeletons made of chitin-derived plates, sometimes reinforced with calcium carbonate, and jointed limbs.
- **Cambrian**- A period of time in the Paleozoic Era from 541 to 485 million years ago.
- **Carboniferous**- A period of time in the Paleozoic Era from 359 to 300 million years ago.
- **Cenozoic**- An era of time in the Phanerozoic Eon from 65 million years ago until now.
- **Chordate**- Any member of the animal phylum Chordata, including sea squirts, lancet fish, and vertebrates (such as lampreys, sharks, tuna, frogs, lizards, chickens, and people). All chordates have, at least at some point in their life cycle, a notochord, a long, flexible rod, usually made of cartilage, or, in the case of most vertebrates, cartilage and bone, running down the back from head to tail, directly beneath the neural tube.
- **Cnidarian**- Any member of the animal phylum Cnidaria, such as jellyfish, box jellies, Portuguese Man'o'war, sea anemones, coral and the parasitic myxozoans. Cnidarians are usually radially symmetrical, and have unique, venom-injecting stinging cells called "cnidocytes."
- **Cretaceous**- The last period of time in the Mesozoic Era, from 144 to 66 million years ago.
- **Devonian-** A period of time in the Paleozoic Era from 414 to 360 million years ago.
- **Ediacaran-** The last period of time in the Precambrian Eon from 635 to 542 million years ago.
- **Eocene-** A period of time in the Cenozoic Era from 55 to 33 million years ago.
- **Fauna-** In an ecological context, "fauna" refers to the animal components of an ecosystem.
- **Formation-** In a geological or paleontological context, a formation is a group of rock layers.
- **Gnathostome-** A gnathostome is any vertebrate chordate with a moveable jaw (or had an ancestor with one).
- **Holocene-** A period of time in the Cenozoic Era from 12,000 years ago until now.
- ***Incertae sedis-*** A Latin phrase literally meaning "uncertain seat." *"Incertae sedis"* is a term in classification used to refer to a species or group whose relationships with related organisms are unclear or poorly defined.
- **Jurassic-** The second period of time in the Mesozoic Era, from 199 to 145 million years ago.
- **Mesozoic-** An era of time in the Phanerozoic Eon from 249 to 66 million years ago.
- **Miocene-** A period of time in the Cenozoic Era from 23 to 5 million years ago.

- **Mollusk**- Any member of the animal phylum Mollusca, including snails, clams, squid, octopuses, tusk shells and chitons. Most mollusks have a calcium carbonate shell, and a toothed, file-like tongue called a radula. All mollusks have a cape-like organ, the mantle, which usually secretes the shell, and houses breathing organs, and a nervous system.
- **Nekton**- Any aquatic animal that lives either entirely or almost entirely in the water column, and relies on its own swimming or propulsion abilities to keep and move itself in and around the water column. Anchovies, porpoises and ichthyosaurs are examples of nekton.
- **Neogene**- The second third of the Cenozoic Era, comprising of the Miocene and the Pliocene periods.
- **Oligocene**- A period of time in the Cenozoic Era from 33 to 23 million years ago.
- **Ordovician**- A period of time in the Paleozoic Era from 484 to 440 million years ago.
- **Paleocene**- A period of time in the Cenozoic Era from 65 to 55 million years ago.
- **Paleogene**- The first third of the Cenozoic Era, comprising of the Paleocene, Eocene, and Oligocene.
- **Paleozoic**- An era of time in the Phanerozoic Eon from 249 to 66 million years ago.
- **Permian**- The last period of time in the Paleozoic Era, the time of "The Great Dying," or most severe of all known extinction events, from 299 to 250 million years ago.
- **Pharynx**- A structure in the throat of many animals located directly behind the mouth or oral chamber. In vertebrates, it often houses breathing structures, like gills.
- **Plankton**- An organism that uses water currents and waterflow to as its primary means of transportation in the water column because it is either too small to move long distances by its own power, or lacks the ability to propel itself entirely. Sargassum seaweed and jellyfish are two varieties of plankton.
- **Pleistocene**- A period of time in the Cenozoic Era from 3 million years ago until 12 thousand years ago.
- **Pliocene**- A period of time in the Cenozoic Era from 5 to 3 million years ago.
- **Quaternary**- The last third of the Cenozoic Era, comprising of the Pleistocene and the Holocene periods.
- **Terrestrial**- Living on land.
- **Triassic**- The first period of time in the Mesozoic Era, from 249 to 200 million years ago.

Name   Sigil Proarticulatan

Species	*Praecambridium sigillum*
Phylum	Proarticulata
Class	Cephalozoa
Family	Yorgiidae
Size	No more than 5 mm by 4 mm
Time Period	Late Ediacaran of the Precambrian, 555 million years ago
Location	Ediacara Hills, in the northern Flinders Rang, South Australia, Australia.

Comments

The Sigil Proarticulatan, *Praecambridium sigillum*, is a tiny, arthropod-like organism from the Late Precambrian of the Ediacara Hills, back when the state of South Australia was a shallow sea. The generic name refers to the probable mollusk, *Cambridium*, in reference to the bumps of the segmentation resemble the muscle-attachment scars on the inner surface of the mollusk's shell.

When the proarticulatan *Vendia* was discovered, it was thought to be an arthropod due to its blatant segmentation, and vaguely trilobite-like shape. Similarities between it and *Praecambridium* were noted, and then, it, too, was regarded as a "Precambrian arthropod." At least, it was until newer, better preserved fossils showed that *Vendia* was a proarticulatan like *Dickinsonia* and *Yorgia*.

Currently, the sigil proarticulatan is thought to be closely related to the much larger proarticulatan, *Yorgia*, which is found mostly in Russia, and rarely, Australia.

Name   Hugmonster

Species	*Amplectobelua symbrachiata*
Phylum	?Arthropoda
Class	Dinocaridida
Order	Radiodonta
Suborder	Anomalocarida
Family	Amplectobeluidae
Size	Body length without trailing furci estimated to be up to 1 meter
Time Period	"Stage 3" of the Cambrian Period, 515 million years ago
Location	Chengjiang County, Yunnan Province, China
Comments	The Hugmonster, *Amplectobelua symbrachiata*, is one of several anomalocarids from the Maotianshan Fauna in Chengjiang County (the blurry creature in the background is a related horror, *Omnidens*, known from an enormous, detached mouth-plate).

The hugmonster is known primarily from several detached grasping appendages. They differ from those of the better known *Anomalocaris* in that those of the hugmonster have a large spine on the fourth segment. This enlarged spine would have allowed the hugmonster to better grasp prey similar to how a crab or scorpion grabs prey with their pincers. The hugmonster further differs from *Anomalocaris* in that the hugmonster has the last pair of fins modified into a pair of trailing, streamer-like appendages termed "furci." Rare whole-body fossils show that the living animal was up to 1 meter in length.

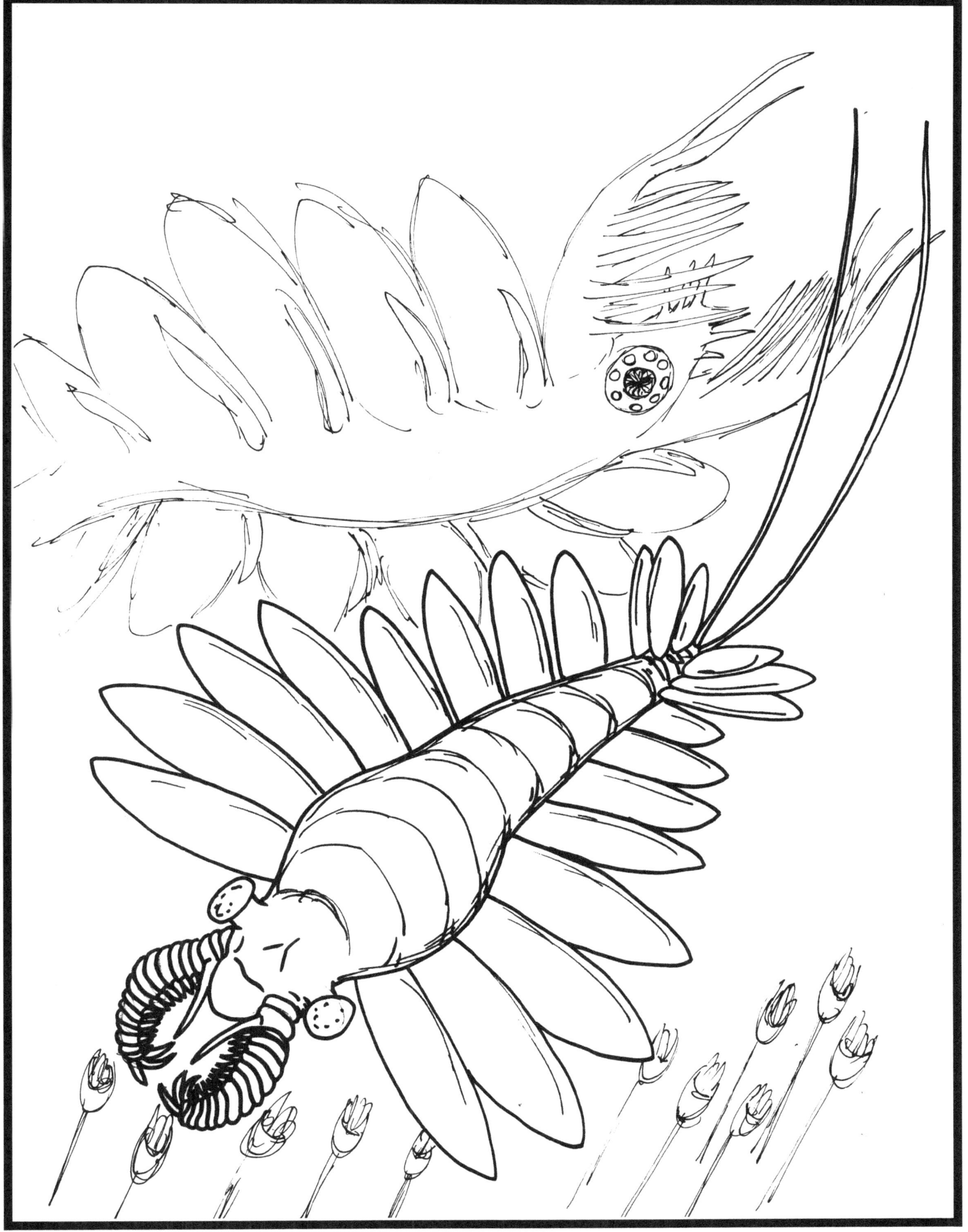

Name

Broadbrowed Stygian Helmetrilobite

Species	*Stygina latrifrons*
Phylum	Arthropoda
Class	Trilobita
Order	Corynexochida
Family	Styginidae
Size	Up to 3 centimeters in length
Time Period	Middle to Late Ordovician, about 467 million years ago
Location	Norway and Sweden
Comments	

The Broadbrowed Stygian Helmetrilobite, *Stygina latrifrons*, is one of several species of stygian helmetrilobites that flourished throughout the Middle to Late Ordovician of what is now Western Europe (the broadbrowed's fossils being found in what is now Norway and Sweden).

Styginid helmetrilobites were a diverse group of corynexochids that lived in oceans during the Ordovician and Silurian Periods. The first styginids discovered by humans, including the broadbrowed, were originally thought to be asaphid trilobites related to the Indistinctobites of the genus *Asaphus*. Over a century's worth of examinations would see the styginids shuffled into and out of various trilobite orders until they were placed within Corynexochida.

Much like their lookalikes, the indistinctobites, and numerous other, pillbug-like trilobites, the stygian helmetrilobites, including the broadbrowed, were benthic mudgrubbers that probably hunted for worms and other burrowing animals. The small eyes of the stygians suggest they lived in deep, dark, or murky water.

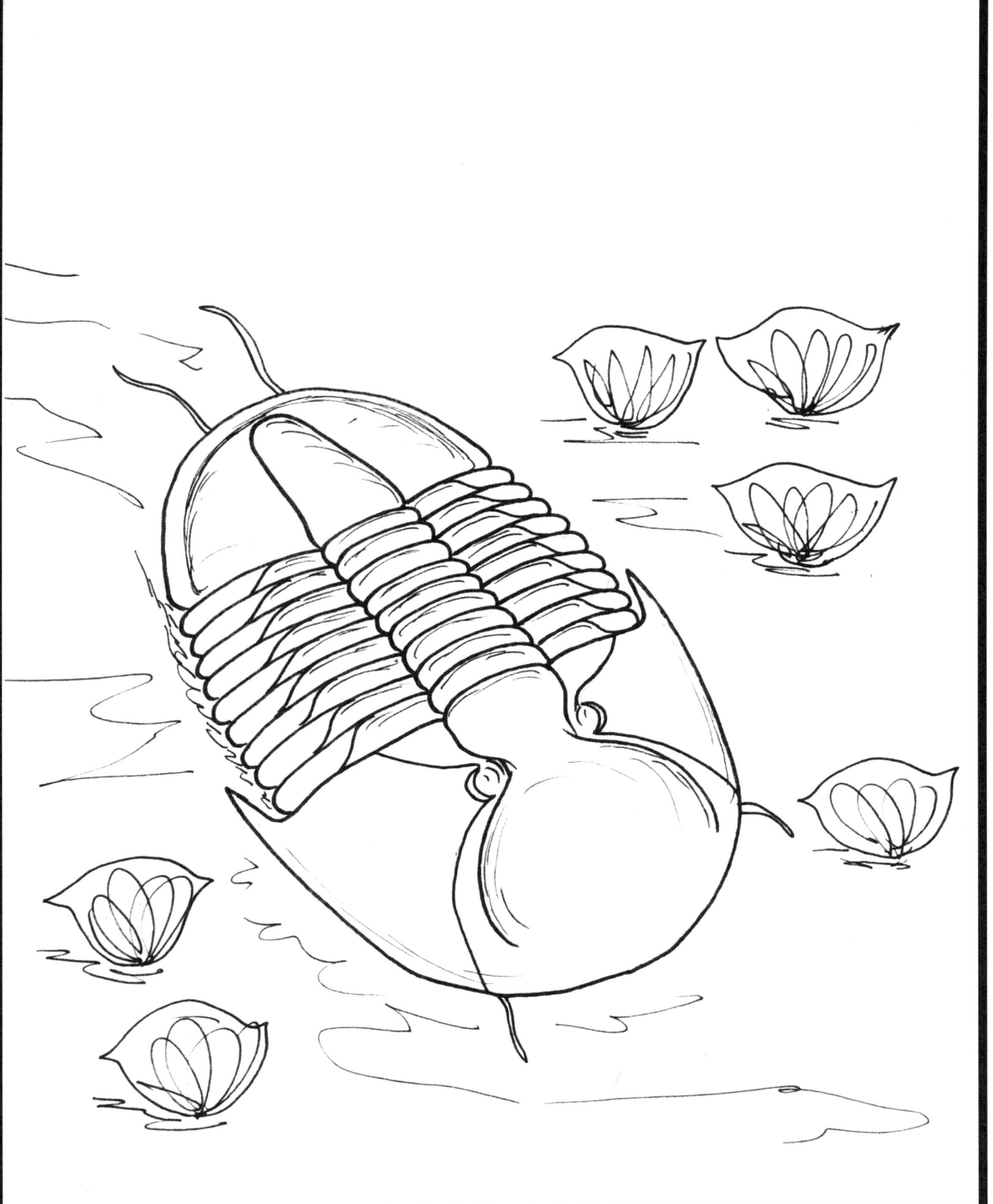

Name	Forbes' Phishbone Phacopid
Species	*Deiphon forbesi*
Phylum	Arthropoda
Class	Trilobita
Order	Phacopida
Family	Cheiruridae
Size	Up to 3 centimeters in length
Time Period	Wenlock epoch of the Middle Silurian, 433 million years ago
Location	In England, the Wenlock Limestone of Dudley and Wallsall, and the Wenlock Shale of Malvern Tunnel. Bohemia, and Sweden

Comments

The Forbes' Phishbone Phacopid, *Deiphon forbesi*, is a peculiar phacopid trilobite from Silurian Europe, discovered by French-turned-Czech paleontologist Joachim Barrande. Barrande named this fish-skeleton-esque creature after British naturalist, Edward Forbes, in order to commemorate their personal friendship (Forbes would return this sentiment by naming another trilobite *Deiphon barrandei*).

The glabellum is large, globular, and covered in wart-like tubercules. The pleurae, or side-extensions of the exoskeleton covering the legs, are modified into rib-like structures, and the cheeks are modified into long, recurved spines. The segments of the pygidium, too, are modified into long spines. The function(s) of these modifications are unknown, but have been speculated about for decades. A popular idea is that the the phishbone was a pelagic or planktonic swimmer that may have pursued prey in the water column. This idea falls apart when one understands that the rib-like spines would not aid in streamlining, and the round, warty glabellum would impair its hydrodynamics for swimming.

Most likely, it crawled along the seafloor, and hunted for prey, which it may have stored in its large glabellum.

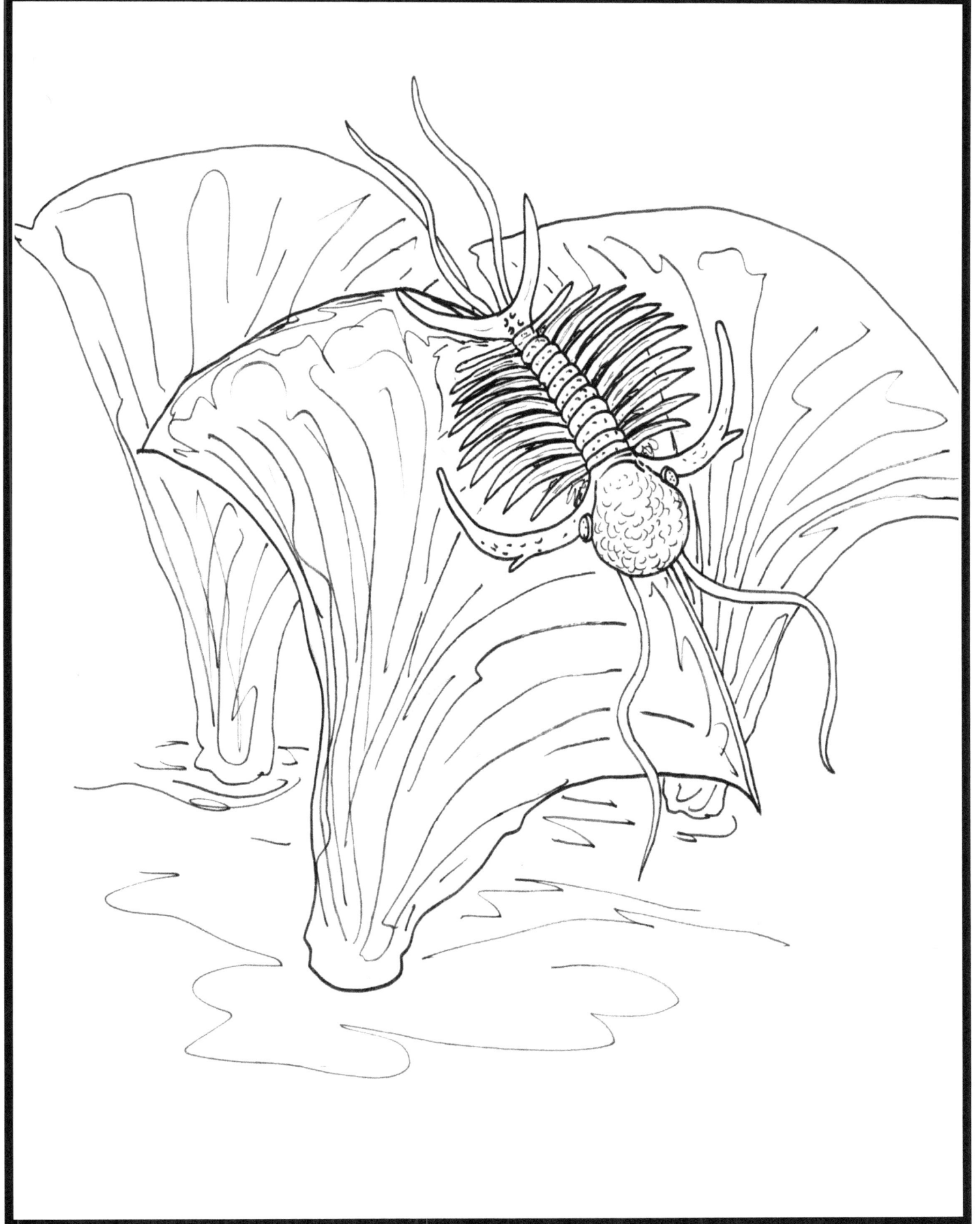

Name	Monstrous Twinhorned Toothriblobite
Species	*Dicranurus monstrosus*
Phylum	Arthropoda
Class	Trilobita
Order	Odontopleurida
Family	Odontopleuridae
Size	Up to 6 centimeters in length and width with spines, body length without spines about 2 to 2.5 centimeters.
Time Period	Late Pragian to Early Emsian epochs of the Middle Devonian, 408 to 395 million years ago
Location	Morocco and Bohemia
Comments	The Monstrous Twinhorned Toothriblobite, also known as the (Monstrous) Ramshorn Trilobite, *Dicranurus monstrosus*, is probably the most famous odontopleurid trilobite, as its iconic, curling head-horns for which the genus is named are unmistakable.

In the case of the monstrous, the horns are the largest, most-curving in the genus. The horns' purpose are, as with the spines of all fabulously spinose trilobites, the source of much speculation. The most plausible hypothesis states that the lateral spines helped redistributed the animal's weight so that it would not sink into soft mud, while both the lateral and head spines discouraged gnathostome vertebrate predators, such as the arthrodire placoderm, *Atlantidosteus*, shown here.

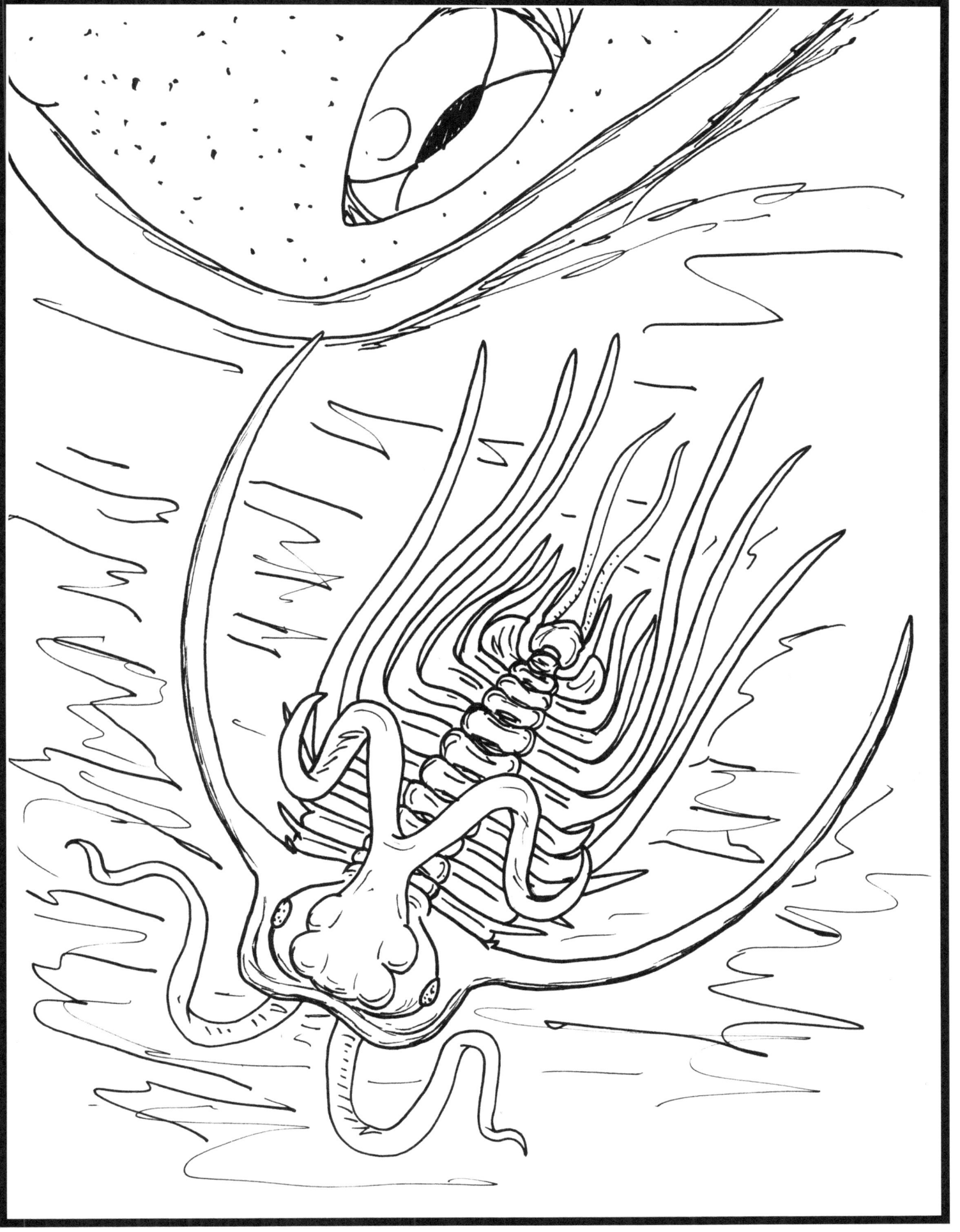

Name

(Eugene) Richardson's Mazon Creek Centipede

Species	*Mazoscolopendra richardsoni*
Phylum	Arthropoda
Subphylum	Myriapoda
Class	Chilopoda
Order	Scolopendromorpha
Size	Estimated to be over 5 centimeters in length
Time Period	Middle Pennsylvanian epoch of the Carboniferous, about 300 million years ago
Location	Braidwood Biota of Mazon Creek, either Will or Kankakee County, Illinois
Comments	The (Dr Eugene) Richardson's Mazon Creek Centipede, *Mazoscolopendra richardsoni*, is one of two scolopendromorph centipedes known only from Paleozoic-aged fossils (the other being *Palenarthrus impressus*). As the generic name refers, fossils of the Mazon Creek Fauna of Carboniferous Illinois, where it dwelled in the leaf litter of a clubmoss-dominated tropical rainforest. It is very similar to modern-day scolopendromorph centipedes, and probably occupied a similar lifestyle of searching for other invertebrates to overpower, envenomate and devour, such as this hapless, primitive house centipede, *Latzellia primordialis*, shown here in the clutches of a Richardson's Mazon Creek centipede. Both centipedes are compared to part of the leg of the fringed giant millipede, *Arthropleura cristata*.

Name   Blackwater Prowler

Species	*Surcaudalus rostratus*
Phylum	Chordata
Class	Chondrichthyes
Subclass	Elasmobranchii
Infraclass	Euselachii
Size	Up to 20 centimeters long: adult size unknown
Time Period	Middle Capitanian Epoch (Late Kazanian age) of the Late Permian, about 260 million years ago
Location	Rangal Coal Measures of the Late Permian Blackwater Group, Queensland, Australia.
Comments	The Blackwater Prowler, *Surcaudalus rostratus*, is a freshwater sort-of-true shark (i.e., an elasmobranch of Euselachii, but not a ray in Batoidea) that lived in a large, freshwater lake in what is now Queensland, Australia, around 260 million years ago. This lake had a diverse ecosystem with numerous species of bony fishes. So far, the blackwater prowler is known only from several fossils of small, juvenile individuals: no adults have yet been found.

Living individuals would have probably looked similar to the modern-day nurse sharks, *Gingylostoma sp.,* but with a proportionally larger tail, and prominent spines in the dorsal fins. Or, at least, they would look similar to nurse shark pups.

Here, a blackwater prowler is carrying off an individual of *Bowngriphus perphlegis*, a mysterious invertebrate denizen of the Blackwater Group lakes of unknown affinities.

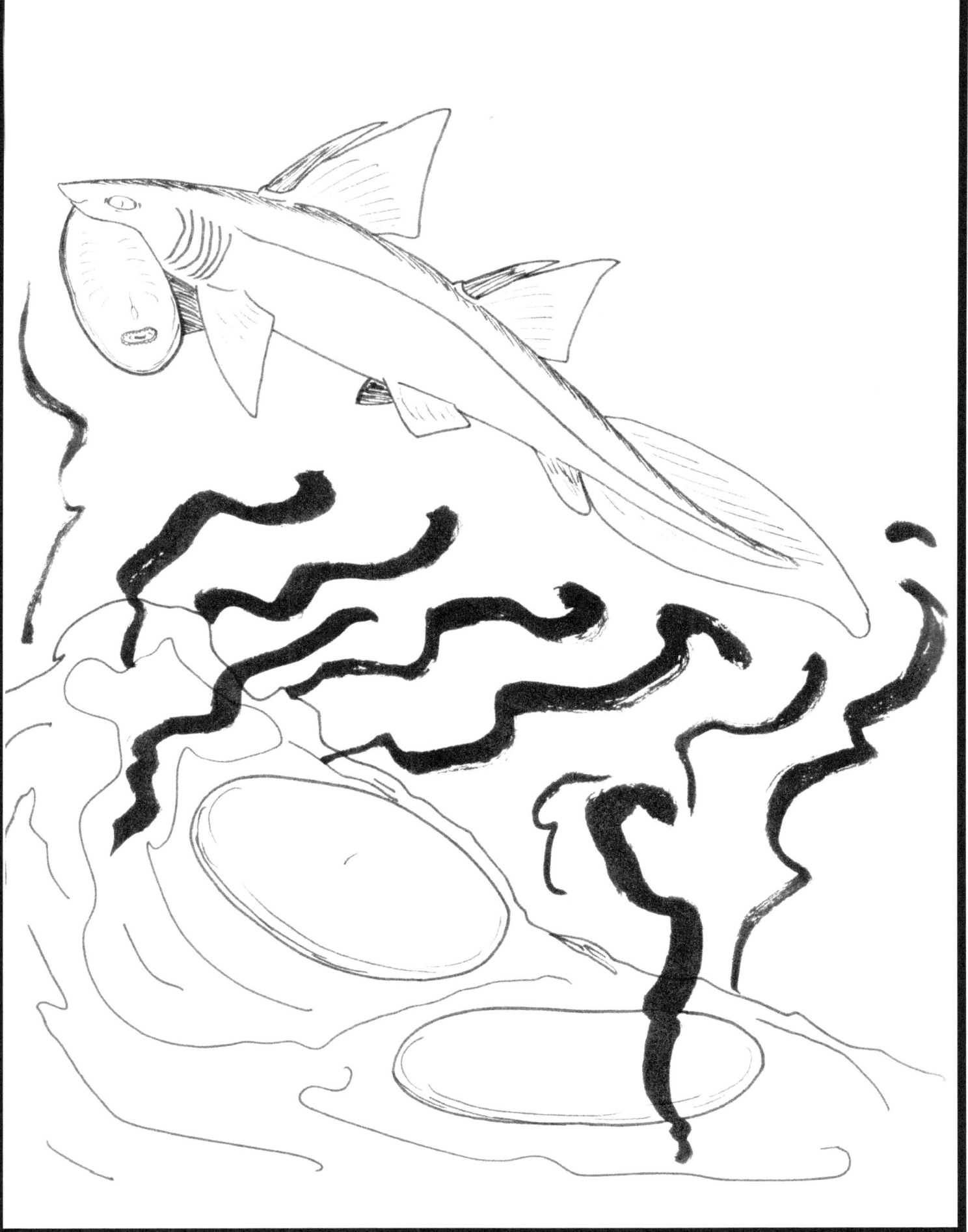

Name	Rebelacanth
Species	*Rebellatrix divaricerca*
Phylum	Chordata
Class	Osteichthyes
Subclass	Sarcopterygii
Order	Coelacanthiformes
Family	Rebellatricidae
Size	Estimated to be up to 130 centimeters in length.
Time Period	Early Olenekian Epoch of the Early Triassic, about 250 million years ago.
Location	Sulphur Mountain Formation, Wapiti Lack Provincial Park, British Columbia
Comments	The Rebelacanth, *Rebellatrix divaricerca*, is the earliest known large coelacanthid after the Permian-Triassic Extinction Event, and represents the biggest deviation in the typical coelacanthid bodyplan since the coelacanthids' evolutionary renaissance during the Mississippian portion of the Carboniferous.
	During the early Triassic in British Columbia, there was a large lake that supported a diverse fish fauna. The rebelacanth evolved possibly in response to this, and had the posterior dorsal fin, and the anal fin modified into a homocercal second tailfin that would have allowed it to have bursts of speed while pursuing prey, similar to how many modern-day open water sharks (which would not appear until the Jurassic or Cretaceous) hunt fish.

Name	Lameer's Dawn Cicada
Species	*Eocicada lameeri*
Phylum	Arthropoda
Class	Insecta
Order	Hemiptera
Suborder	Auchenorrhyncha
Infraorder	Cicadomorpha
Superfamily	Palaeontinoidea
Family	Palaeontinidae
Size	Wingspan maybe up to 10 centimeters
Time Period	Late Tithonian Epoch of the Late Jurassic Period, 149 to 145 million years ago
Location	Central Europe
Comments	The Lameer's Dawn Cicada, *Eocicada lameeri*, is an extinct hemipteran insect, or plant louse, from what is now Central Europe. It is known primarily from wings that detached from their owners after death, though, a few fossils feature whole individuals, suggesting a large (for a plant louse) insect with a wingspan of maybe 10 centimeters. The dawn cicada cold be easily distinguished from the latter-appearing (true) cicadas by how its head was much much smaller. Whether or not the dawn cicada or its relatives in family Palaeontinidae could make noise like modern cicadas is currently unknown.
	Like all plant lice, the Lameer's dawn cicada drank sap from plants. It remains unknown if it preferred a specific host plant or had several.

Name Jamaican Torc Clam

Species	*Titanosarcolites giganteus*
Phylum	Mollusca
Class	Bivalvia
Order	Hippuritoida
Family	Antilocaprinidae
Size	Shell diameter up to 1 meter in adults.
Time Period	Maastrichtian Cretaceous, 70 to 66 million years ago
Location	Jamaica and Cuba
Comments	The Jamaican Torc Clam, *Titanosarcolites giganteus*, is a gigantic rudist clam, and formed bioherm-type reefs (reefs formed from great, collected heaps of individuals of the reef-building species) in a shallow sea in what is now Cuba and Jamaica during the Late Cretaceous. The shells of all rudist clams are modified pipes, some being pillor-shaped, others squashed as boxes, pots or cones, and still others, like the Jamaican torc clam and its relatives, have their shells modified into coiled ribbons. In most rudists, one valve of their shell is modified into a much smaller lid which protected the animal from predators. In the case of the torc clams and their relatives, both valves are equal size. In all Cretaceous-aged rudists, the living animal only occupied a very small living chamber, which was, in the case of the torc clam, located in the center of the shell where the two valves joined.
	As mentioned earlier, the Jamaican torc clam formed bioherm-type reefs in what is now Jamaica and Cuba, where their fossils are found, where several other species of rudists, including the star-shaped *Biradiolites jamaicensis*, and the clustered *Praebarrettia sparcilirata*, coexisted.

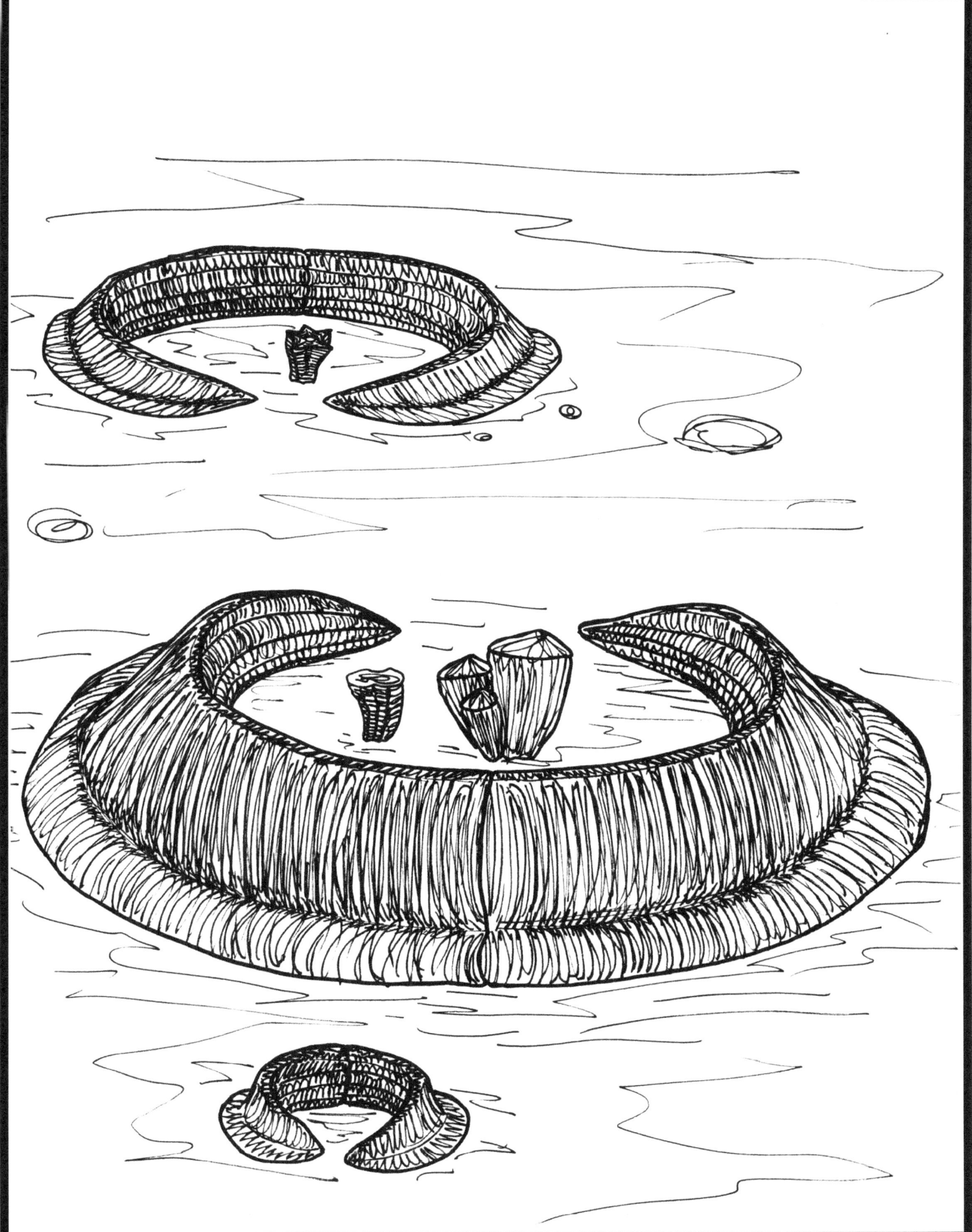

Name	Chinese Whale Mesonychid
Species	*Sinonyx jiashanensis*
Phylum	Chordata
Class	Mammalia
Order	Mesonychia
Family	Mesonychidae
Size	Similar in size to a modern-day grey wolf
Time Period	Thanetian Epoch of the Late Paleocene, about 56 million years ago
Location	Anhui Province, China
Comments	The Chinese Whale Mesonychid, *Sinonyx jiashanensis*, is a medium-sized mesonychid from the Late Paleocene of Anhui Province, China. As with most other mesonychids, the Chinese whale mesonychid was a superficially wolf-like animal that preyed on and or scavenged other animals, probably the many primitive ungulates that lived in the area at the time. The Chinese whale mesonychid's sagittal crest (where the upper jaw muscles attach to the skull) is greatly enlarged, even more so than other mesonychids, suggesting a devastatingly powerful bite, especially when the narrow, multi-pronged shearing molars and carnassal teeth are accounted for.

When the "mesonychid-to-cetacean" theory was still in vogue, it was observed that the Chinese whale mesonychid shared many dental and cranial anatomical features with primitive whales such as *Pakicetus* and *Ambulocetus*, leading researchers to proclaim that *Sinonyx* was a missing link between mesonychians and cetaceans. However, with newer DNA comparisons showing that cetaceans are actually artiodactyls closely related to hippopotamids, and the fact that primitive whales have the diagnostic pulley-astralagus wrist of artiodactyls, which all mesonychians, the Chinese whale mesonychid, included, lack , the Chinese whale mesonychid's whale-like features are now thought to represent an episode of convergent evolution.

Name	Maohu
Species	*Maofelis cantonensis*
Phylum	Chordata
Class	Mammalia
Order	Carnivora
Suborder	Feliformia
Family	Nimravidae
Size	Skull about 19 centimeters long
Time Period	Early Priabonian Epoch of the Late Eocene, about 37 million years ago
Location	Youganwou Formation of Maoming Basin, Guandong Province, China
Comments	The Maohu, 茂虎, *Maofelis cantonensis*, is the first Asian nimravid carnivoran known from a mostly complete skull (Asian nimravids, in contrast to the excellent fossil records in Europe and North America, are known mostly from teeth and fragments). The maohu lived during near the start of the Late Eocene in what is now Guandong Province, China, near Guandong City. It is a basal nimravid more primitive than either *Nimravus,* or *Hoplophoneus*. The maohu would have probably been about the size of a puma, but much stockier (if one goes by the physiques of other nimravids), prominent sabre-teeth (which give the nimravids their collective common name of "false sabre-teeth").

Name	Quercy Ourstigre
Species	*Quercylurus major*
Phylum	Chordata
Class	Mammalia
Order	Carnivora
Suborder	Feliformia
Family	Nimravidae
Size	Estimated to be as large as a brown bear
Time Period	Early Oligocene, about 30 million years ago
Location	Oligocene region of the Quercy Phosphorites Formation, France, and Carrascosa del Campo, Spain
Comments	The Quercy Ourstigre, *Quercylurus major*, is a primitive nimravid (not as primitive as the maohu, though) from the Early Oligocene of the Iberian Peninsula. It is known only from fragments and some teeth that both suggest a tremendous predatory animal that would have easily subdued large prey.
	Here we see the bear-sized, bear-like Quercy ourstigre compared to its leopard-like relative, *Eusmilus bidentatus*, and the owl *Sophiornis quercynus*.

Name	Palmate-Toothed Sansan Tigre
Species	*Sansanosmilus palmidens*
Phylum	Chordata
Class	Mammalia
Order	Carnivora
Suborder	Feliformia
Family	Barbourofelidae
Size	Estimated body length of about 150 centimeters
Time Period	Late Burdigalian to Early Messenian epochs ("Orleanian to Astaracian") of Early to Late Miocene, 13 to 11 million years ago
Location	France and China
Comments	The Palmate-Toothed Sansan Tigre, or Palmate-Toothed Sansanhu, *Sansanosmilus palmidens*, is a leopard-sized, modest-fanged species of barbourofelid feliform carnivoran that ranged from France into China during the Miocene period. Compared to the contemporary true felid, *Pseudaelurus*, and to later barbourofelids like *Barbourofelis*, the palmate-toothed sansan tigre had stocky limbs and a plantigrade stance.
	Despite having moderately long fangs, especially when compared to *Barbourofelis* or *Eusmilus*, it is quite obvious that the palmate-toothed Sansan tigre could easily tackle most small to medium-sized prey animals, though, probably not the well-defended French necropangolin, *Necromanis fraconica*, shown here.

Name   Issiore Lynx

Species   *Lynx issiodorensis*

Phylum   Chordata

Class   Mammalia

Order   Carnivora

Suborder   Feliformia

Family   Felidae

Size   Similar in size to modern lynxes

Time Period Villafranchian Age, from the Late Pliocene to Middle Pleistocene, 3 to 1 million years ago

Location   Western and Central Europe

Comments   The Issiore Lynx, *Lynx issiodorensis*, is an extinct species of lynx ancestral to all other lynxes and bobcats. The first fossils were found in Pliocene-aged strata near Issiore, France, though, more fossils have been found in Spain and Italy, as well.

The Issiore lynx would have resembled modern lynxes, though, it would have had more "normal" cat-like proportions, i.e., a bigger head, slightly longer body, shorter and more robust limbs.

Here, the Issiore lynx is depicted pursing the extinct hare, *Oryctolagus layensis* in typical lynx-fashion.

Name

South American Sabre-toothed Tiger

Species	*Smilodon populator*
Phylum	Chordata
Class	Mammalia
Order	Carnivora
Family	Felidae
Subfamily	Machairodontinae
Tribe	Smilodontini
Size	At least 120 centimeters at the shoulder, comparible in size to a Siberian tiger
Time Period	Late Pleistocene to Early Holocene, from 1 million to 10,000 years ago.
Location	South America
Comments	The South American, or Devastating Sabre-toothed Tiger, *Smilodon populator*, is a tiger-sized sabre-toothed cat from the Late Pleistocene to Early Holocene of South America, fossils of which have been found from Venezuela to Southern Argetina.

S. populator was the first member of the genus *Smilodon* described. *S. populator* is thought to have evolved from the Gracile Sabre-toothed Tiger, *S. gracilis*, a jaguar-sized animal that lived in early Pleistocene Eastern North America which would also give rise to the later, lion-sized Western Sabre-toothed Tiger, *S. fatalis*, of La Brea Tarpits fame.

Because most of the indigenous South American ungulates became extinct just prior to the Great American Faunal Interchange, the South American sabre-toothed tiger was an ambush predator that most likely preyed on the numerous horses, deer, and camelids that replaced the South American ungulates. *S. populator* also competed with big cats, such as the jaguar, *Panthera onca* (shown here), the American lion, *P. (leo) atrox*, and the cougar, *Puma concolor*. The South American sabre-toothed tiger did not compete with the other indigenous South American sabre-toothed cat, *Homotherium venezuelensis*, as that species went extinct in the Middle Pleistocene before *S. populator* appears in the fossil record during the Late Pleistocene.

Name

Tongan Giant Skink

Species	*Tachygia microlepis*
Phylum	Chordata
Class	Reptilia
Order	Squamata
Suborder	Sauria
Family	Scincidae
Size	Over 30 centimeters in length
Time Period	Holocene, only living specimens seen by Europeans collected in April or May of 1827 AD
Location	Island of Tongatapu, in the Pacific Ocean
Comments	

The Tongan Giant, or Ground Skink, *Tachygia microlepis*, is the second-largest lizard endemic to the islands of Tonga in Polynesia. The largest endemic lizard was the Tongan Giant Iguana, *Brachylophus gibbonsi*, shown partly here in the immediate background.

The only living, or perhaps freshly dead Tongan giant skinks seen by outsiders were a pair collected by native Tongans apparently for trade with the French naturalists Jean René Quoy and Joseph Paul Gaimard on behalf of their master, Captain J. S. C. Duman d'Urville, when Captain d'Urville's ship, *l'Astrolabe*, almost ran aground on a Tongan reef during the spring of 1827. The lizard was a plump, ashy-grey-brown creature with small scales, and currently, both of the only known specimens currently reside in jars of alcohol in the basement of the Muséum National d'Hiostire Naturelle, Paris, France.

Nothing is known about its habits, as it has never been seen alive since, even after repeated searches. The cause of its extinction is assumed to be due to humans, either destroying habitat, or introducing predatory animals like rats, cats and dogs.

Bibliography

- Agust, Jordi, and Mauricio Antón. *Mammoths, sabertooths, and hominids: 65 million years of mammalian evolution in Europe*. Columbia University Press, 2005.
- Averianov, Alexander, et al. "First nimravid skull from Asia." *Scientific reports*6 (2016): 25812.
- Cherin, Marco, Dawid Adam Iurino, and Raffaele Sardella. "New well-preserved material of Lynx issiodorensis valdarnensis (Felidae, Mammalia) from the Early Pleistocene of Pantalla (central Italy)." *Boll. Soc. Paleontol. Ital*52.10 (2013).
- Edgecombe, Gregory D. "Chilopoda–the fossil history." *Treatise on zoology—anatomy, taxonomy, biology. The Myriapoda* 1 (2011): 355-361.
- Flannery, Tim Fridtjof, and Peter Schouten. *A gap in nature: discovering the world's extinct animals*. Atlantic Monthly Press, 2001.
- Fortey, Richard A. "Lifestyles of the trilobites." *American scientist* 92.5 (2004): 446-453.
- Geisler, Jonathan H., and Mark D. Uhen. "Morphological support for a close relationship between hippos and whales." *Journal of Vertebrate Paleontology*23.4 (2003): 991-996.
- Ginsburg, Léonard. "Révision taxonomique des Nimravini (Carnivora Felidae) de l'Oligocène des Phosphorites du Quercy." *Bull. Mus. Nat. d'Hist. Natur. 4e sér* 1 (1979): 35-49.
- GLAESSNER, MARTIN F., and MARY WADE. "Praecambridium-a primitive arthropod." *Lethaia* 4.1 (1971): 71-77.
- Hou, Xian-guang, et al. "Anomalocaridids." *The Cambrian Fossils of Chengjiang, China: The Flowering of Early Animal Life* (2017): 154-161.
- Ivantsov, Andrei Yu. "Vendian animals in the Phylum Proarticulata." *Abstr. Int. Symp."The Rise and Fall of the Vendian Biota," IGSP Project*. Vol. 493. 2004.
- Kurtén, Björn. "The lynx from Etouaires, Lynx issiodorensis (Croizet & Jobert), late Pliocene." *Annales Zoologici Fennici*. Finnish Academy of Sciences, Societas Scientiarum Fennica, Societas pro Fauna et Flora Fennica and Societas Biologica Fennica Vanamo, 1978.
- Leu, M. R. "A LATE PERMIAN FRESH-WATER SHARK FROM EASTERN AUSTRALIA." *Palaeontology* 32 (1989): 265-286.
- Levi-Setti, Riccardo. *The Trilobite Book: A Visual Journey*. University of Chicago Press, 2014.
- Morlo, Michael. "New remains of Barbourofelidae (Mammalia, Carnivora) from the Miocene of Southern Germany: implications for the history of barbourofelid migrations." *Beiträge zur Paläontologie* 30 (2006): 339-346.
- Mundel, Peter. "The centipedes (Chilopoda) of the Mazon Creek." *Mazon Creek Fossils. Academic Press, New York* (1979): 361-378.
- Peigne, Stephane. "Systematic review of European Nimravinae (Mammalia, Carnivora, Nimravidae) and the phylogenetic relationships of Palaeogene Nimravidae." *Zoologica*

scripta 32.3 (2003): 199-229.

- Ritchie, Alexander, and Gregory D. Edgecombe. "An odontogriphid from the Upper Permian of Australia." *Palaeontology* 44.5 (2001): 861-874.
- Salter, John William. *A monograph of the British trilobites from the Cambrian, Silurian, and Devonian formations.* Cambridge University Press, 2015.
- Shear, W. A. "The fossil record and evolution of the Myriapoda." *Arthropod relationships.* Springer Netherlands, 1998. 211-219.
- Shi, HUANG Xue. "Mammalian remains from the late Paleocene of Jiashan, Anhui." *Vertebrata PalAsiatica* 1 (2003): 003.
- Skelton, P. W., S. K. Donovan, and H. L. Dixon. "Palaeoecology of the late Cretaceous rudist Titanosarcolites giganteus (Whitfield) in Jamaica and Cuba: fiction and fact." *Contributions to Geology, UWI, Mona* 1 (1994): 27.
- Skelton, P. W., S. K. Donovan, and H. L. Dixon. "Palaeoecology of the giant antillean rudist bivalve Titanosarcolites giganteus (Whitfield)." *Third International Conference on Rudists, México DF: Proceedings.* 1993.
- Skjeseth, Steinar. "The Middle Ordovician of the Oslo region, Norway. 5." *The trilobite family Styginidae. Norsk geologisk tidsskrift* 35 (1955): 9-28.
- Turner, Alan. *National Geographic Prehistoric Mammals.* National Geographic, 2004.
- Wang, Bo, et al. "Palaeontinidae (Insecta: Hemiptera: Cicadomorpha) from the Upper Jurassic Solnhofen Limestone of Germany and their phylogenetic significance." *Geological Magazine* 147.4 (2010): 570-580.
- Wendruff, Andrew J., and Mark VH Wilson. "A fork-tailed coelacanth, Rebellatrix divaricerca, gen. et sp. nov.(Actinistia, Rebellatricidae, fam. nov.), from the Lower Triassic of Western Canada." *Journal of Vertebrate Paleontology* 32.3 (2012): 499-511.
- Whittard, W. F. "LII.—A revision of the trilobite genera *Deiphon* and *Onycopyge.*" *Journal of Natural History* 14.83 (1934): 505-533.
- Whittington, Harry B. "*Stygina, Eobronteus* (Ordovician Styginidae, Trilobita): Morphology, classification, and affinities of Illaenidae." *Journal of Paleontology* 74.5 (2000): 879-889.
- Whittington, Harry B. "Type and other species of Odontopleuridae (Trilobita)." *Journal of Paleontology* (1956): 504-520.
- Wittry, Jack. The Mazon Creek Fossil Fauna. Esconi, 2012.
- Wootton, Robin J. "Reconstructing insect flight performance from fossil evidence." *Acta zoologica cracoviensia* 46.Suppl. (2003).
- Xian-Guang, Hou, Jan Bergström, and Per Ahlberg. "Anomalocaris and other large animals in the Lower Cambrian Chengjiang fauna of southwest China." *Gfi* 117.3 (1995): 163-183.
- Zhou, Xiaoyuan. *Evolution of Paleocene-Eocene Mesonychidae (Mammalia: Mesonychia).* Diss. 1995.

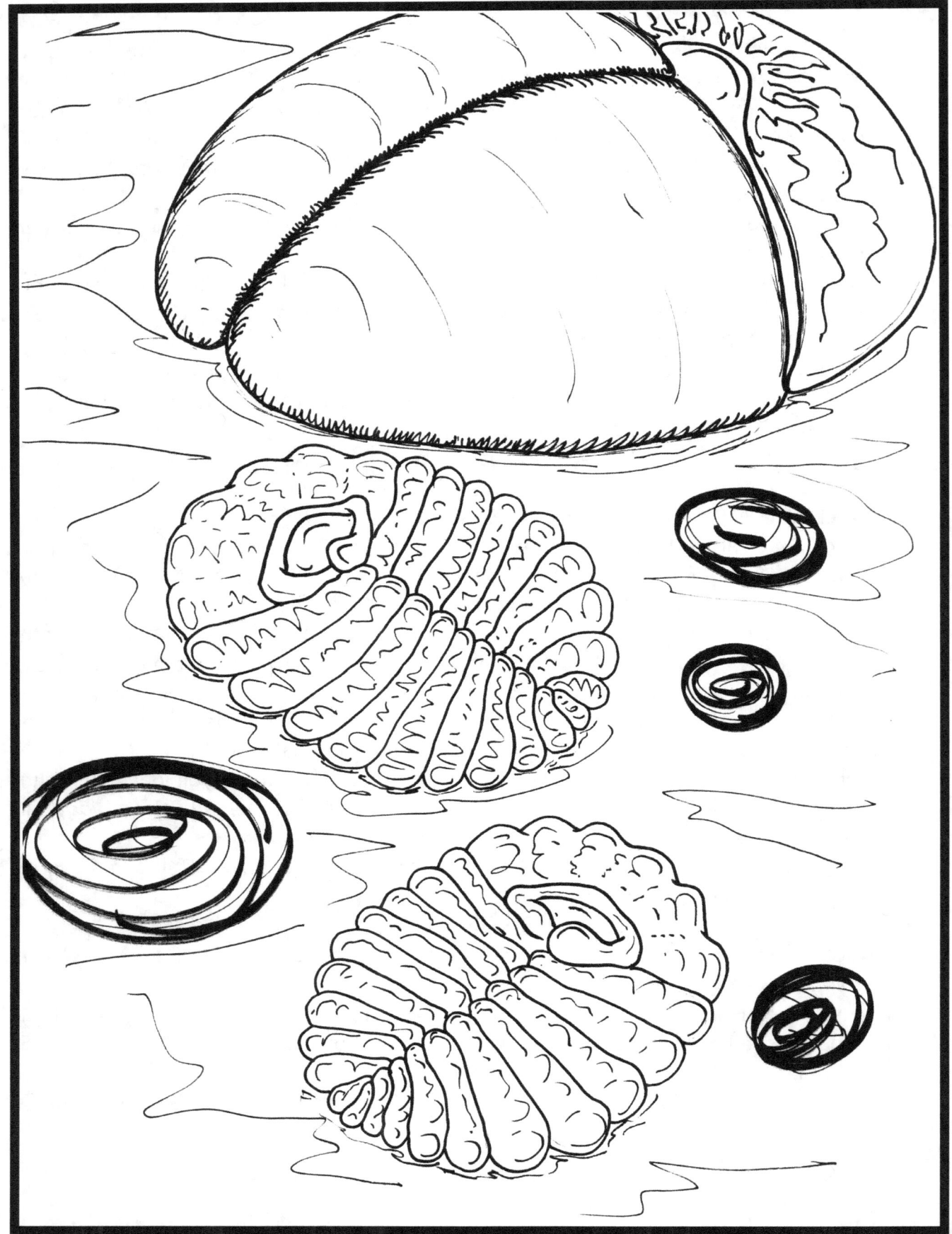

About the Artist

Stanton F. Fink is a student of Biology and Chinese Medicine, and makes a hobby of drawing monsters and researching flowers, arcane-looking creatures, prehistoric animals, fish, reptiles, birds and the occasional, really grotesque fungal fruiting body.

Stanton grew up and went to school in California and is currently living, drawing, and gardening in Oregon.

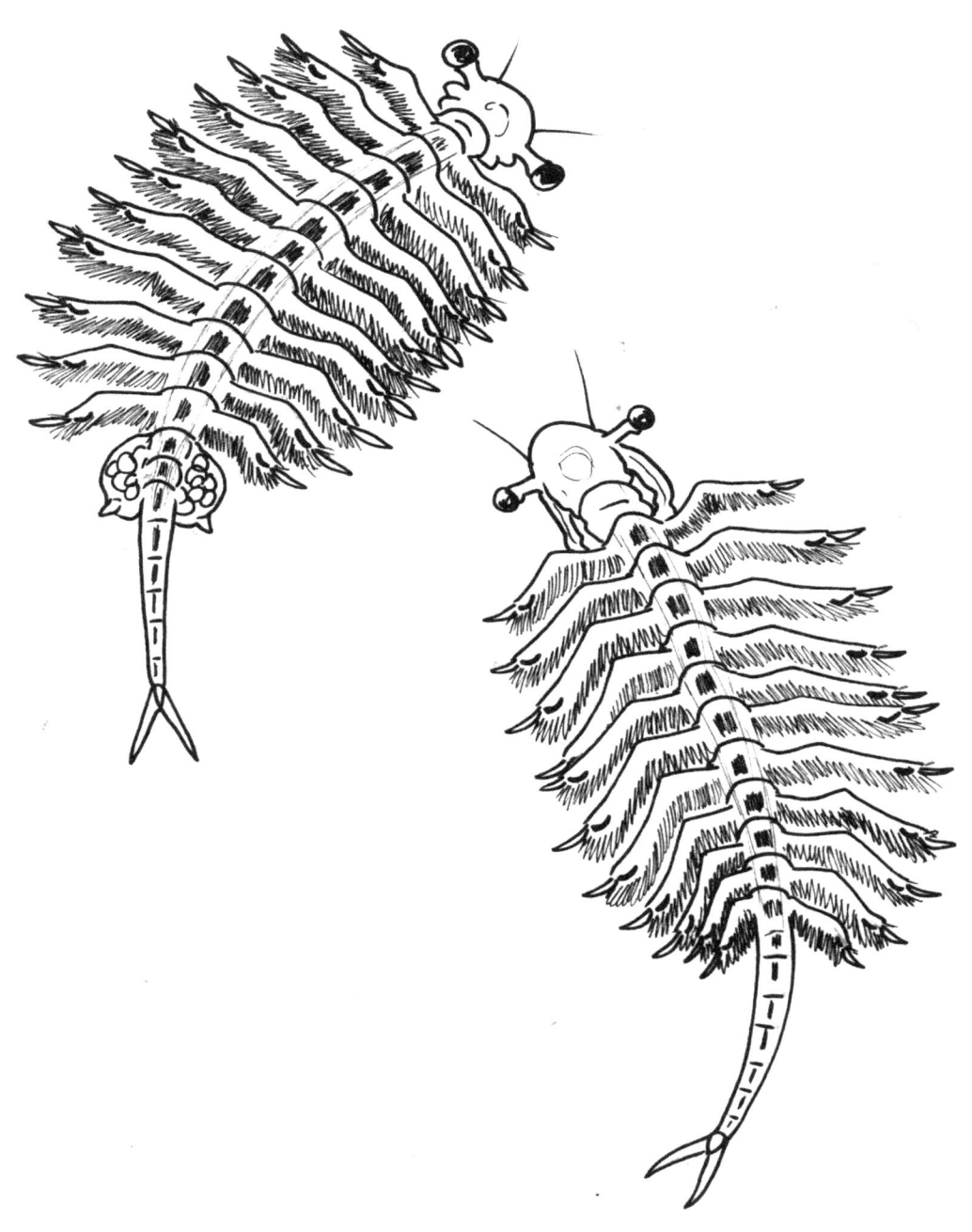

www.ingramcontent.com/pod-product-compliance
Lightning Source LLC
Chambersburg PA
CBHW081126280526
45787CB00007B/2992